Overcoming the Challenge of Singleness
(Practical Solutions from the Book of Ruth)

Gideon & Faith Bakare

Unless otherwise specified, all Bible quotations in English are from the New Revised Standard Version (NRSV 1989).

Copyright © 2015 by Gideon & Faith Bakare

First published in 2015 Divine Solution Publication

ISBN 978-0-9932745-0-3

Do you have any question? Do you want to receive prayers? Would you like to share with us about how this book has blessed your life? We respect your privacy. Please e-mail: solutionoutreach@yahoo.co.uk or divsolmin1@yahoo.com

Printed by Divine Solution Publication
United Kingdom
+44 7533599030

Dedication

We dedicate this book to single Christians worldwide. We also dedicate it to all our spiritual sons and daughters who are still trusting God for their life partners. You are always in our thoughts and prayers. Your day of celebration is closer than before in Jesus name.

Acknowledgement

We bless the Lord Almighty for the vision, direction and inspiration to write this book on an important subject bothering many single Christians around the world. We are thankful to the Lord for providing health, strength and ministry opportunities.

Since many people were involved in one way or another in the success of this book, we would like to publicly express our deep appreciation for their efforts. Many thanks to the leadership of the Kingdom Business Partners for encouraging us to write on this topic so that we can effectively reach out to our younger generation who are seeking help about their future.

We thank Dr. Emmanuel Tukasi for agreeing to write the foreword. We appreciate the effort of Sister Temitope Lawal for thoroughly reading through the manuscript and suggesting what could make it better. We also thank Dr. Yaya Obozua, Pastor Peter Emordi and Sister Idy Omi for their helpful suggestions. We are especially indebted to our children for their sacrifice and understanding.

Finally, the Lord has surrounded us with relatives, friends, dynamic Church members, spiritual sons and daughters. You have all prayed and encouraged us in the process of writing this book. You have contributed to the success of this publication. We cannot mention all your names here, but your reward with the Lord is sure. God bless you.

Gideon & Faith Bakare
March 2015.

Foreword

We live in a world where many youths now want to delay marriage because of career and other personal reasons. The increase in the number of unmarried singles who are desperate to marry is worrisome for both Christians and non-Christians. The people of the world have suggested cohabitation and other mundane solutions, but these temporary approaches have left many in a state of devastation. Gideon and Faith have looked into a specific book of the Bible to offer some insights in this book.

I would like to recommend 'Overcoming the Challenge of Singleness' for three reasons:

First, the book offers a balance between an academic and practical reading of the book of Ruth. Gideon Bakare is a biblical theologian with a pastoral heart. His imaginative reflection on the biblical text is deep and powerful. This allows me to spot the sections he may have written. Faith Bakare, on the other hand, is a guidance counselor. She has been able to offer some practical applications with the use of contemporary equivalents. Reading the book of Ruth from these perspectives focusing on marriage offers a fresh reading.

Second, the authors have the credentials to write on the topic after many years of pastoral counselling and youth ministry. They also went through the stage of singleness before they got married. Hence, they have the competence to put forward some biblical and pastoral counselling suggestions in this book. Pastors, parents, singles and other readers will find them useful.

Third, the principles highlighted for singles in chapters one and two are relevant. The relationship lessons in chapter three will surely reassure single Christians to wait upon the Lord. It is amazing that Gideon and Faith can glean so much from the book of Ruth.

I am convinced this book will open the door of marital breakthrough for many. It will also educate many people on how to come to terms with their singleness.

Dr. Emmanuel O. Tukasi
United Kingdom

Reflection

Ten Commandments for Unmarried Christian Singles

My husband put in place what he called 'Ten Commandments for Christian Bachelors and Spinsters' in 1992. They later re-appeared in our book titled 'The Christian Youths and Pre-Marital Sex.' All the commandments are relevant to the story of Ruth and Boaz in the book of Ruth. They link up easily with the various parts of chapters 1, 2 and 3 of this book. These commandments are still relevant today.

1. You shall not marry an unbeliever. If you do so, you have Satan as your father-in-law (2 Cor. 6:14–17).

2. You shall not rush into marriage. If you 'rush in', you will eventually 'rush out.' Try to exercise the patience that works. It can work for you too (Psalm 27:14; Isaiah 49:23b).

3. You shall not engage yourself in premarital sex. It is a sin against God and your body. It also devalues you before your prospective partner. Therefore, wait until your wedding day (1 Cor. 6:14–20; 7:8–9).

4. Remember to seek God's face before falling in love with any lady or man (Gen. 24:12–15). Pray now, so that you would not pray compulsory prayers in the future.

5. You shall not go into marriage when you are not physically, financially, emotionally and spiritually ripe for it (1 Tim. 3:3–4).

6. You shall not neglect the counsel of your godly parents, pastors and elderly ones concerning marriage (Gen. 28:1–7).

7. You shall not marry a lady or man you do not love wholeheartedly. Allow your love for each other to flourish naturally. Do not force yourself on any man or woman (Gen. 29:17–18).

8. You shall not marry a lady who does not respect you or a man who does not value you (1 Peter 3:1–7; Eph. 5:23).

9. You shall not go into marriage with a lady or man you do not know about his or her family background. Learn lessons from the mistakes of Esau, Samson and Solomon (Gen. 26:34; Judges 16:4; 1 Kings 11:3).

10. You shall not marry a lady or man who is inconsistent and unfaithful to you during courtship (1 Cor. 15:33). It is a danger signal, WATCH OUT!

Mrs. O.F. Bakare
January 2015

Contents

Introduction

Stories about young men and women who were involved in marital relationships abound in the Scripture. In the book of Genesis, Isaac loved Rebecca so much that he was comforted through her (Gen. 26:67). Jacob fell in love with Rachel to the extent that he waited and worked for another seven years in order to marry her (Gen. 29:11, 15–20). In Exodus, Moses was in a romantic relationship with Zipporah (Exo. 2:21–22; 18:3–4). The book of Ruth tells us about the marriage between Ruth and Boaz (Ruth 4:7–17). The chemistry and passion between David and Abigail was recorded in 1 Samuel 25: 39–42. In Matthew, Joseph and Mary were deeply in love (Matt. 1:18–25). There are many more examples from other books of the Bible, but our focus here is on the book of Ruth.

Ruth means 'mercy,' 'friendship,' 'refreshment' or 'comfort.' The author of the book of Ruth did not reveal his or her identity. Rabbinic tradition suggests that Prophet Samuel wrote it. Scholars have suggested other names ranging from David, Solomon, Naomi and many others (Block, 1999: 597; Gottwald, 1985: 555). However, some of the suggestions are only speculations without evidence. Furthermore, Keil & Delitzsch suggest that the story of Ruth happened during the time when

Gideon was judge (ca. 1180–1140 B.C.) over Israel (Keil & Delitzsch, 1887: 466).

The book of Ruth is about a journey of faith. Biblical scholars have read it focusing on important themes such as loyalty, faith, salvation or redemption, the providential works of God, God's faithfulness in providing rest for His people and many more. According to the NET Bible, one of the important messages of the book of Ruth is that 'God cares for needy people like Naomi and Ruth; He is their ally in this chaotic world. He richly rewards people like Ruth and Boaz who demonstrate sacrificial love and in so doing become his instruments in helping the needy. God's rewards for those who sacrificially love others sometimes exceed their wildest imagination and transcend their lifetime.' Similarly, Reed notes that 'the Lord is faithful in His business of loving, superintending, and providentially caring for His people' (1985: 418). This book only focuses on the idea of marriage in the book of Ruth.

There are many characters in the book of Ruth. They include Elimelech (My God is king), Naomi (fair or pleasant), Chilion, Mahlon, Orpah, Ruth, Boaz and others. However, we want to examine the book of Ruth from the perspective of Ruth and Boaz focusing on dating, relationship, courtship and marriage. The book of Ruth is short with 89 verses, yet we insist that this beautiful and interesting story is loaded with many materials on marriage.

The original idea for this book began during our Bible study session at Evangelical Church Winning All (ECWA) Eastham,

London. We spent several months exploring the book of Ruth and the theological messages in it. Then, my wife and I resolved one evening that we could glean more from the book. We began to re-read the book of Ruth from the perspective of marriage and relationship. This book is the product of our reflection.

Our method of reading the book of Ruth is very simple. We have used our marriage and counselling lenses to explore the topic of relationship in the book of Ruth (with reference to Ruth and Boaz only). We found some relevant principles for getting a life partner. Therefore, we encourage the reader to prayerfully digest the principles in this book and apply them where necessary.

There are three categories of singles that we want to address in this book:

The first are the unmarried singles. They are matured for marriage, but they are still unmarried. They have a desire to get married but no one is asking for their hands in marriage or no one is accepting their marriage proposal. They are ready for marriage but they are concerned about the prospect of meeting the right person (s).

The second are the widows and widowers. They were once married but their spouses have died. According to the Paul's instruction, they are free to re-marry if they wish to do so (1Cor. 7:8–9).

The third are the separated or divorced singles. Some were once legally married but their relationships hit the rock. Others have co-habited and had children outside wedlock before they realised that they were with the wrong person. Many of them are single fathers and mothers facing the challenge of parenting alone.

The purpose of this book is to show that contemporary youths can learn some lessons for from the book of Ruth on how to overcome the challenge of not getting a life partner. Are you currently looking for love and you do not know how to go about it? Have you tried so hard to get a life partner without positive result? You are not alone. God is about to write the next chapter of your life. You can overcome the challenge of not getting a partner. The principles in this book will help you to stand out among others. Are you in a relationship and things are not going towards the right direction? This book offers some valuable insights. It helps you to rediscover yourself and understand the fact that God is working for your good even in your state of singleness.

Are you genuinely seeking for a life partner? We encourage you to allow God to transform you through the message of this book. This book does not answer all the questions about singleness and choosing a life partner. The scope of our investigation is limited to the biblical principles for overcoming singleness that we found in the book of Ruth. A general study on choosing a life partner is therefore available elsewhere (Bakare, 2000; Jackson, 2009).

The Bible was silent about the wife and children (marital status) of Boaz. He was presented as a single man. He was definitely older than Ruth. In Israel, a man of his age, wealth and status would have been married. He was probably a childless widower at that time. There may be other probabilities, but we are not sure. Ruth on the other hand was presented as a single woman. She was the widow of Mahlon who followed Naomi (her mother-in-law) from Moab to Bethlehem in Israel (Ruth 4:10). She was free to remarry according to the Law of Moses.

Solution Prayer Points

- Lord I enter your gate with thanksgiving and your court with praise in Jesus name.
- Lord I ask for forgiveness concerning my past and present sins in Jesus name.
- Heavenly father, open my eyes to see the specific message that you have for me in this book in Jesus name.
- I receive the grace to start and finish reading this book in Jesus name.
- I declare that I shall be the first beneficiary of this book in Jesus name.
- I declare that my day of celebration is closer than before in Jesus name.
- The story of my life will have a happy ending in Jesus name.
- Oh Lord, help me to see beyond my current circumstances in Jesus name.
- I refuse to take relationship and marriage shortcuts in Jesus name.
- Help me to reflect on your special love and plan for my life in Jesus name.
- Let my life bear witness in the world of darkness in Jesus name.
- Help me to always remember that taking a godly path may not be easy, but it leads to eternal satisfaction.

Chapter 1

Biblical Principles for Getting a Husband

This chapter focuses on the life, character and actions of Ruth (the Moabite). It explores the things that made her attractive to the men of her time. We shall read the book of Ruth from the perspective of Ruth so that Christian single ladies can draw lots of inspiration from her life. She is now a model for young women seeking for a life partner in a godly way.

The principle of regeneration

Getting married among the Israelites went beyond the physical, emotional and social reasons. There was a spiritual dimension to it. Ruth said:

> Do not press me to leave you or to turn back from following you! Where you go, I will go; where you lodge, I will lodge; your people shall be my people, and your God my God. Where you die, I will die—there will I be buried. May the Lord do thus and so to me, and more as well, if even death parts me from you (Ruth 1:16–17)!

Ruth renounced the Moabite gods and embraced Yahweh (the holy one of Israel). She was regenerated. She took her spirituality seriously. You must also renounce the works of darkness and worldly pleasures. You must accept Jesus Christ as your Lord and personal saviour. This should come first before any other thing. Are you born again? Are you connected with God? Has your name been written in the book of life?

The principle of commitment

Ruth was totally committed to helping Naomi. She 'clung to her' (Ruth 1:14) and refused to return to Moab (Ruth 1:16–17). She demonstrated the same level of commitment when they got to Bethlehem. Your prospective husband is also looking at your commitment to God and the needy in the community.

The principle of hard work

According to God's instruction in the Law of Moses, all farmers in Israel should not harvest everything on field. They must leave the corners of their fields for the poor or needy, aliens, widows and orphans. This would allow them to glean enough food for survival (Lev. 19:9–10; 23:22). Therefore, Ruth was qualified for gleaning as a widow and a foreigner.

Ruth was not a lazy person (Ruth 2:2). She was a hardworking woman. She took the first initiative by requesting Naomi to allow her to go and glean from the field. Ruth was a good example of hard work and industry. The Bible confirms that she was on her feet from early morning until the evening 'without resting even for a moment' (Ruth 2:7b, 2:17a). She followed the harvesters tumbling to glean from their leftovers throughout the harvest season. You must also distinguish yourself in one area or the other. Even in an agrarian society, Ruth was able to find something for herself. She was not a liability to her prospective husband. You too should go out and look for a job. You must make good use of all the opportunities available to you today. You must be productive and proactive.

The principle of good appearance
Ruth washed and anointed herself. She put on her best clothes on the night she met Boaz at the threshing floor (Ruth 3:3a). She did not underdress or overdress. She dressed moderately. Of course, what a man is looking for in woman goes beyond beauty but good appearance could be the starting point for your prospective husband. It may serve as an attention getter before he begins to see other virtues in you. Therefore, you must look good and presentable in the public. You must package and perfume yourself regularly. In addition to your dressing, smile wherever you are. This is an important factor that you cannot rule out in your search for a husband. This principle worked for Ruth and it is still working today.

There is another aspect of good appearance that we must mention. Nowadays, we appear socially, not just in person, but also through social media. We show our appearance on Facebook page, Twitter account, YouTube videos, WhatsApp groups, the things we say on our online sites and the pictures we put out there. For example, a picture (appearance) on Facebook may attract a man to a lady, and vice versa. Therefore, it is fundamental that the pictures you put on social media are decorous. They are all part of your appearance that could attract or discourage your prospective partner.

The principle of obedience to God's guidance

Ruth allowed herself to be guided by the Lord. She did not disobey. Finding herself in the field belonging to Boaz, who was a relative of Elimelech was not accidental (Ruth 3:3). It was a divine arrangement made possible by Ruth's obedience. You must be obedient to the leading of the Holy Spirit if you want your path to cross with the husband that God has ordained for your life. There is a reason for everyone that God has allowed you to come in contact with.

The principle of excellence

Ruth stood out among other women in Bethlehem at that time. She exhibited the spirit of excellence. She was exceptional in all that she did. She was dedicated and diligent. This made it possible for Boaz to take notice of her. Boaz asked, 'to whom does this young woman belong' (Ruth 2:5)? You too must be outstanding in whatever you are doing at the moment (schooling, singing, helping, teaching etc.). This is one of the ways to easily get noticed by your prospective husband.

The principle of politeness

Ruth was polite in her approach (Ruth 2:7). She made an appeal to be allowed to glean after the harvesters. Her virtue of politeness was displayed throughout the book of Ruth. Ruth's politeness yielded three results: First, she was treated politely in return. Second, her request to glean after the harvesters was granted. Three, she got more than what she expected. She got a lovely husband in the end.

The principle of chemistry

The word 'chemistry' in the context of relationship has puzzled relationship experts. It is an emotional connection or attraction between two people (especially a man and woman). It may or may not be sexual. It is a special impulse that makes two people to want to be together or see each other regularly. There was chemistry between Ruth and Boaz when they met each other (Ruth 2:5). There was a feeling within Ruth that she has met the right man. Chemistry matters in every relationship. How did you feel when you met the young man at work or after the Church service?

Online dating is another dimension to the principle of chemistry. Of course there has been huge debates among Christians about the usefulness of online dating. Those who dislike it felt that online activities have opened the way for scams, identity theft impersonation and other criminal acts. A non-believer may even disguise as a Christian. Those who like the idea on the other hand felt Christian online dating is among the current social way of engagement. Hence, it is worthy of exploration. We encourage individual reader to decide what is best for them.

Nowadays individuals do enter into online relationships where some sort of chemistry develops by exchanging words and pictures over Christian online dating sites, Facebook and other forms of media. Some online relationships started and died online, and some have developed into relationships in the real world after a short or long period.

The principle of following godly parental instructions

Ruth religiously followed Naomi's godly parental instructions. All of them are well documented in Ruth 3:1–4. Then, Ruth replied, 'all that you tell me I will do' (Ruth 3:5). You also have a duty to prayerfully follow the advice and instructions of your parents that are in line with the word of God concerning marriage.

The principle of availability (being at the right place)

Ruth did not hide herself with self-pity in the house of Naomi. She went out to showcase her virtues before Boaz saw her. The threshing floor was the meeting place for Ruth and Boaz (Ruth 3:3b). It was a public place. Being at the right environment is very essential. Ruth made herself available at the threshing floor. God will crown your effort of looking for a partner with success but He will not come down from heaven. In most cases, God will send somebody. You also have a responsibility to do what Ruth did by mixing with godly people. You must learn to be at the right place. Your threshing floor can be anywhere as long as the name of the Lord is glorified. You may meet your life partner at the Church, school, bus or train station, inside the bus or train, place of work, friend's house, youth camp, your neighborhood and at a sport competition etc. Then, your prospective husband will take notice of you. Are you at the right place? Are you hanging out with the right people?

The principle of selecting the right time

Naomi instructed Ruth, 'do not make yourself known to the man until he has finished eating and drinking' (Ruth 3:3c). Ruth was on target because she selected the right time. When you do the right thing at the wrong time, it can lead to disaster. It is always good to take the right step at the right time concerning your marriage. It must not be too early or too late. The Bible says, 'he has made everything beautiful in its time' (Eccl. 3:11). You need a discerning spirit in order to recognise when God wants you to make the next move. There is time and season for everything in the world including marriage proposal. Ruth acted at the appointed time. Then, everything continued to fall in place for her.

The principle of using the right method

There is always an alternative to the way you do things. Therefore you need to use the right method. Ruth used a specific method by asking Boaz to be the kinsman redeemer. This is acceptable within the Jewish culture. A childless widow is allowed to remarry and raise children within the family. It is the responsibility of the closest relative. The Jewish culture also allows the woman to make a proposition in this situation. This raises the question whether a lady is allowed to propose to a man? The answer to this question would vary from one culture to another. For example, most African and Asian communities would prefer a man to propose to a woman. However, some European communities don't really worry about the one who makes the proposition. The method that worked for some people may not work for others. This method worked for Ruth and

Boaz. You will have to prayerfully trust God for the right method.

The principle of expressing faith

Ruth did not know that she could ever be married again until she took the step of faith. You need a measure of faith to be able to step out to look for a life partner. Right faith will motivate you to continue to trust God for a husband.

The principle of having the right attitude

Ruth did not see challenges. She saw opportunities. She did not see test. She saw the testimonies that would emerge at the end. Having the right attitude helps you to stand firm in times of adversity looking onto Jesus as the author and finisher of your faith. It helps you to learn to stand up in the power of God and conquer your current state of singleness. A right attitude also helps you to say, 'waiting does not mean I will never get it.' Waiting on the Lord for a husband does not make you a failure, giving up easily does. Developing a right attitude will help you to remember that God's plan for your marital life was already decided before you were born. Do you have the right attitude towards God? Do you have the right attitude towards yourself? Do you have the right attitude towards others? Your attitude must change for better if you want to successfully find a husband.

The principle of adaptability and good human relation

Ruth's level of adaptability and human relation were excellent. She was a foreigner. Yet she was able to adapt quickly and settle into the Israelite community. She learnt very fast and related well with the young women on the field (Ruth 2: 17–18). Those who want to marry people from other cultures, tribes or nationalities should have some understanding about the cultural values of their partners. What is acceptable in your culture may be offensive to the culture of your partner. For example, calling people by their first name is acceptable among the Western Europeans. This could be understood as lack of respect in another culture (especially Africans and Asians).

The principle of kindness
Ruth showed kindness by leaving her country (Moab) and following Naomi back to Bethlehem (Ruth 1: 8–9). She also offered to go out and work in order to look after Naomi in her old age. 'So she gleaned in the field until evening. Then she beat out what she had gleaned, and it was about an ephah of barley. She picked it up and came into the town, and her mother-in-law saw how much she had gleaned. Then she took out and gave her what was left over after she herself had been satisfied' (Ruth 2: 17–18).

Ruth also showed kindness to Boaz in two ways. First, she expressed interest and willingness to stay with Boaz by serving as his maidservant and by gleaning in his fields. Second, she expressed interest and willingness to marry Boaz (Ruth 3:10). This is another evidence of her love and loyalty to Naomi so that the name of Elimelech, Chilion and Mahlon may not be cut off from their kindred (Ruth 4:9–10). No wonder, when Ruth gave birth to Obed, the people said that 'Naomi had a son' (Ruth 4:9–16).

According to Gideon & Faith Bakare, Ruth was initially a divine connection for the economic and financial survival of Naomi.

She later realised that Naomi was also her divine connection for marriage (Bakare, 2014: 20). Remember that no act of kindness will go unrewarded. It will come back to you. Therefore, the person you've shown kindness can turn around to be the source of your marital solution.

The principle of good character
Ruth's character was of high quality. She was a blessing to everyone who came in contact with her. Her humility was very outstanding. 'Then she fell prostrate, with her face to the ground, and said to him, "Why have I found favor in your sight, that you should take notice of me, when I am a foreigner" (Ruth 2: 10)? Good character is one of virtues that god-fearing young men are looking for. It must not be missing in your life.

The principle of good speech
Ruth spoke wisely. She carefully chose her words. 'Then she said, "May I continue to find favor in your sight, my lord, for you have comforted me and spoken kindly to your servant, even though I am not one of your servants"' (Ruth 2:13). Words are powerful. They can open the gate for you to have access to your future husband. They can also shut the door to a prospective husband. Boaz was overwhelmed with Ruth's nice words. Are your words attracting people to you or sending them away?

The principle of chastity and integrity
Ruth had an option to be sleeping around with the servants of Boaz in order to guarantee her survival. She however resolved to keep herself pure. Boaz testified that Ruth has 'not gone after young men, whether poor or rich' (Ruth 3:10). She was eventually compensated for her integrity. Your state of

singleness is not a license for licentiousness. You must respect yourself if you want people to respect you. Ruth and Boaz developed interest in each other, but they kept themselves pure. Many singles are quick to jump into the bed with their new or prospective partners thinking that sex will solidify their relationships. It has been proven that reverse is the case. Those who do that usually open the way for their prospective partners to cast doubt on their loyalty and fidelity. The strongest relationships always put God at the centre and not sex. Genuine love should be able to say, 'I love you too much. I will not take advantage of you, or cause you pain. I will not ask you to do something you feel is wrong and that you will feel bad about tomorrow.'

The principle of following the right process
Ruth decided to follow the right process by consulting with Boaz to be the kinsman redeemer. The necessary family steps were taken before they made the relationship legal. Ruth also kept herself pure until all the necessary family arrangements were finalised. You need to get the approval of your parents and ensure that proper procedures are followed.

The principle of doing what is humanly possible
Ruth did all she could do as human and left the rest to God. Remember that you cannot start a relationship by force. God will not demand for anything beyond your human capacity. Do your part and leave the rest to God. God has a responsibility to link you up with your future partner. You also have a responsibility to respond to God's leading. Ruth's action models one way by which divine and human actions work together. She did not wait passively for events to happen. She took a step of faith.

The principle of surrendering your life to God

Ruth surrendered her life to the will of God. She did not allow immediate gratification to becloud her sense of judgment. You also have a responsibility to think about the larger picture. You must ignore people's opinion and focus your attention on God.

The principle of prayer

There is no clear indication that Ruth prayed for a husband but we can see the result. The appearance of Boaz in the life of Ruth was an answered prayer. Prayer is one of the vital parts of relating with the God of Israel. One would imagine that Naomi and Ruth prayed to Yahweh every day about their situation and the future of Ruth. They prayed for guidance before Ruth went out to the field (Ruth 2:2). They prayed that Ruth's expression of love for Boaz at the threshing floor would workout well (Ruth 3:1–13). The Lord who answered the prayers of Ruth still answers prayers today. Now is the time to start praying for a life partner. Pray also for God's blessing on the steps you want to take.

The principle of refusing to dwell on the past

Ruth did not allow the pains, failures and mistakes of the past to hunt or hurt her future. The Bible says, 'forget the former things; do not dwell on the past. See, I am doing a new thing! Now it springs up; do you not perceive it? I am making a way in the wilderness and streams in the wasteland' (Isaiah 43:18–19). Ruth's joy was short-lived when she lost her husband. You should not allow your past to hinder what God wants to do in your life.

The principle of submission

Ruth was submissive to the counsel, wisdom and authority of her mother-in-law. She was also submissive to the authority and laws of the Israelites. She displayed a commitment to follow Yahweh and His chosen people. This overwhelmed Boaz and made him to indicate a strong affection for her (Ruth 2:11–17). Are you submissive to God and your parent?

The principle of patience

There is need for you to exercise patience after you have taken all the above steps. It is not the day or week that Ruth got to Bethlehem that she met Boaz. It took some time. There is a tendency for you to want to rush when you are desperately in need of something. Naomi said to Ruth, 'Wait, my daughter, until you learn how the matter turns out, for the man will not rest, but will settle the matter today' (Ruth 3:18). Ruth exercised patience. You too should be patient with God. You should also be patient with the young man as he prayerfully makes a decision on the relationship. Don't rush yourself and the young man.

The principle of leaving, cleaving and becoming one flesh

The final principle in this chapter is leaving, cleaving and becoming one flesh. 'So Boaz took Ruth and she became his wife' (Ruth 4:13). Ruth loved Naomi so much but she is obliged to leave her and move into the house of her husband. Of course, this does not mean you have to abandon your parents, what it implies is that you need a bit of space in order to start a new life as a married woman. May the Lord provide for you a place of rest in Jesus name!

Conclusion

You can expect to get the right result if you follow the above biblical principles for getting a husband in the book of Ruth. Don't worry about the implications of your past on your current situation. Remember that Ruth was previously married before her husband died. She was not a virgin. In addition she was a foreigner. Humanly speaking, her chances were limited. Nevertheless, if God could do it for Ruth, He can do it for you too. You will be married. We shall rejoice with you very soon.

There is a specific husband for you out there. Some years ago, one of our daughters in the Lord came over to study in United Kingdom. She visited a family friend and met another young man there. The young man was so impressed with her attitude and he proposed to her few months later. They both returned to Nigeria at the end of their studies. They are now happily married with two children (a boy and a girl). You will also have the testimony in Jesus name.

Solution Prayer Points

- Finding a godly life partner will not be difficult for me in Jesus name.
- Sustaining a godly relationship will not be difficult for me in Jesus name.
- O Lord, give me a stable and lasting relationship in Jesus name.
- My wedding shall be glorious in the name of Jesus.
- My tears shall be turned to joy in Jesus name.
- Heavenly father, meet my deepest needs in Jesus name.
- Oh Lord, connect me with my destiny partner in Jesus name.
- I rebuke every power that is designed to keep me single forever in Jesus name.

- Henceforth, Christ will be the foundation of my life and relationship in Jesus name.
- Every secret that I need to know to be happily married shall be revealed to me in Jesus name.
- I remove the negative impact that my past is having on my current state of singleness in Jesus name.
- Father Lord, I shall not miss your plan and purpose for my marriage in Jesus name.
- Give me a life partner that will bring comfort to my life in Jesus name.
- Oh Lord, give me a divine connection for marriage in Jesus name.
- No weapon that is fashioned against my marriage will prosper in Jesus name.
- Give me a spirit of discernment to recognise my future partner whenever I meet him in Jesus name.
- Remove every obstacle that is militating against my connection with my life partner in Jesus name.
- Give me the grace to wait for the right person in Jesus name.
- I shall not defile myself before marriage in Jesus name.
- Give me a partner that will be committed to God and our marriage relationship in Jesus name.
- Oh Lord, help me to think protectively and proactively during courtship in Jesus name.
- Oh Lord, help me not to do things that will cause me to regret later in life in Jesus name.
- I will get my marriage relationship right this time around in Jesus name.
- I recover from every negative impact of my past relationships in Jesus name.
- I receive the grace to start afresh in Jesus name.
- I refuse to be discouraged during my search for a life partner in Jesus name.

Chapter 2

Biblical Principles for Getting a Wife

We now turn to re-read the book of Ruth from the perspective of Boaz. We shall examine the life, character, and actions of Boaz. This will help us to see the attributes that distinguished him from other men of his generation. His life offers many principles for unmarried men to consider.

The principle of regeneration

Boaz was a worshipper of Yahweh. He trusted in and committed himself to Yahweh. He had a good understanding about the God of Israel. Hence, it was easier for Ruth to fall in love. Your being born again should be the starting point for your marital journey. In other words, you must be regenerated.

The principle of spirituality

Boaz displayed spirituality and decency in all his connections with Ruth. Similarly, there was no record that he was involved in sexual immorality with anybody in the book of Ruth. He lived his life with fear and reference to the Almighty God. You too must set yourself apart for God before expecting Him to prepare somebody for you. You should focus your attention on God and he will sort out the remaining aspects of your life (including marriage).

The principle of chemistry

As we mentioned earlier, chemistry is the natural feelings that usually draw two people together (especially a man and woman). It is an attraction that makes you feel that you have many things in common with that lady (compatibility). It is a feeling that motivates you to want to talk to or be with that person. There was chemistry between Boaz and Ruth (Ruth 2:5). It was obvious from the first day that Boaz set his eyes on Ruth. This chemistry continued to develop greatly between both of them. How do you feel whenever you talk to the lady you are thinking about? Do you desire to see her again? How often do you want to see her? Can you feel the bounding between you and her?

The principle of observation

Observation is one of the important skills that you need when you are going through the process of choosing a life partner. Boaz took some time to observe the behaviour of many young women in Israel. He also observed Ruth when she arrived from Moab with Naomi (her mother-in-law). He was able to compare and contrast before making any move (Ruth 2:11; 3:11b). He knew the virtues he wanted to see in his future partner. He did not rely solely on the testimonies of others concerning Ruth. His observation helped him to discover that Ruth was a godly and hardworking young woman.

Choosing a life partner is one of the most important decisions you will ever make in your lifetime. It is therefore necessary to carefully observe a lady before you commit yourself into the relationship. For example, what do you know about her family background, godliness, character, attitude towards money, work ethics and behaviour towards members of the opposite sex etc.? Are you satisfied with your assessment? What you see at the observation level will either encourage or discourage your initial interest in the lady.

The principle of discernment
Discernment is the work of the Holy Spirit by which an individual is able to distinguish God's voice in the midst of other voices. It is the ability to understand God's mind. In the context of marriage and relationship, discernment brings about a spiritual connection between a man and a woman. It helps you to recognise that the lady is the right one. Boaz saw many women of good character in Bethlehem, but he was able to know that Ruth was the one. You must be able to exhibit discernment. You need the power of the Holy Spirit to help you in the process of choosing the right partner. There should be a spiritual connection between you and the lady. Remember that the choices you make through the power of the Holy Spirit can lead to blessings far and beyond your wildest dreams.

The principle of thinking before you act
It took Boaz a bit of time to think through the marriage proposal of Ruth. He requested for some time to ponder on the immediate and future implications. He did not take it lightly (Ruth 3:10–13). You must take your decision about marriage seriously. Ask yourself the following questions: Do I really love this lady? Is the spirit of God in me at peace with this relationship? Am I

ready to spend the rest of my life with this person? Am I ready to bear whatever I may encounter in this relationship?

The principle of exercising maturity and leadership
Boaz exercised maturity and leadership throughout the book of Ruth. He was in charge. He was already developing and exhibiting the quality of a good husband before he met Ruth. You should not wait until you meet the woman you want to marry before practicing how to be a good husband. If you are looking for a good wife, you too must be willing to be a good husband.

The principle of waiting patiently
Boaz waited for the best and he got the best. There are two possible reasons why Boaz did not initiate a marriage proposal. First, he may have assumed that Ruth would prefer to marry a younger man that is closer to her age (Ruth 3:10). Second, he understood that he was not the closest eligible male relative (Ruth 3:12) and he does not want to break the law. It is necessary for you to wait patiently upon the Lord for a God-fearing wife. You don't need to rush. There may be pressure from your friends, parents, family members, youth leaders, deacons, pastors and other Church leaders. Some may attempt to push you into a relationship when you are not ready to enter into courtship and marriage. Others may even attempt to match-make you with somebody. However, you must refuse to mount pressure on yourself. You must learn to wait patiently.

The principle of generosity

Boaz was generous towards Ruth on many occasions. He instructed that Ruth should not go to glean in another field. He allowed her to keep close to the young women working for him so that she can keep her eyes on the field and glean bountifully. In addition, he ordered the young men working on the field not to bother her. He also allowed Ruth to go to the vessels and drink from the water the young men have drawn whenever she was thirsty (Ruth 2: 8–9). Moreover, Boaz permitted Ruth to have free launch with the reapers. He even offered to serve her on one occasion. 'At mealtime Boaz said to her, "Come here, and eat some of this bread, and dip your morsel in the sour wine." So she sat beside the reapers, and he heaped up for her some parched grain. She ate until she was satisfied, and she had some left over' (Ruth 2: 14). Similarly, 'when she got up to glean, Boaz instructed his young men, "Let her glean even among the standing sheaves, and do not reproach her. You must also pull out some handfuls for her from the bundles, and leave them for her to glean, and do not rebuke her"' (Ruth 2: 15–16). Boaz also displayed generosity to Ruth at the threshing floor.

> Then he said, "Bring the cloak you are wearing and hold it out." So she held it, and he measured out six measures of barley, and put it on her back; then he went into the city. She came to her mother-in-law, who said, "How did things go with you, my daughter?" Then she told her all that the man had done for her, saying, "He gave me these six measures of barley, for he said, 'Do not go back to your mother-in-law empty-handed'" (Ruth 3:15–18).

Boaz was even more generous on this occasion than before. Frederic Bush suggests that Ruth was given 'an amount that would certainly be possible for a strong young peasant woman, accustomed to such burdens, to carry' (1996:178–179) on that day. Boaz initially did not know that he was preparing the ground and looking after his future wife. In the same vein, the person you have supported or shown favour may end up as your spouse or a partner to your family member.

The principle of financial viability
Boaz was financially viable before he took Ruth to be his wife (Ruth 3:17–18). You should have a job and have a reasonable source of income. This will help you to look after yourself and the new family that you intend to raise.

The principle of hard work
Another principle that is similar to financial viability is hard work. Boaz was not a lazy man. He was enterprising. He had a big farm and employed people to work for him. He regularly visited the field to supervise his workers and provided for their needs (Ruth 2:15–16). Hard work will help you to sustain all that you currently have. It will also motivate you to venture into new horizons for the benefit of your future family.

The principle of taking the first initiative
Boaz took the initiative and went out of his way to make a request that Ruth should not go to another field to glean for the rest of the harvest (Ruth 2: 8–9). Ruth would have gone elsewhere if Boaz did not make the offer. There is need for you to recognise the value and the reward of taking initiative in order to develop a relationship. You should not wait for the lady to make the first move. You may miss the opportunity that God is making available to you. Take initiative, if you are keen about walking in God's blessing and meeting your life partner. The

'perfect moment' may never arrive apart from the one God has already provided. This may require initiating a conversation, offering to help, asking a question, expressing the willingness to go an extra mile in doing what others would not do etc.

The principle of good communication

Boaz was a gentleman with good communication skills. He spoke to people nicely irrespective of their race, gender and status. His words were enriching and comforting. It was easier to predict what sort of husband he would become. He said to Ruth, 'may you be blessed by the Lord, my daughter; this last instance of your loyalty is better than the first; you have not gone after young men, whether poor or rich' (Ruth 3:10). Words are powerful. These words are strong enough to build Ruth's self-esteem. You should only say things that would bless, help, liberate and empower others. A good communication will help prepare the grounds before you make a proposal. It will also sustain your relationship before and after marriage.

The principle of honesty and reliability

Boaz had a track record of honesty and reliability. He displayed it when it mattered. He did not say yes at the threshing floor and later deny his desire for Ruth at the city gate. He also informed Ruth about the challenge or objection that their relationship may face. He was consistent throughout. Boaz said:

> And now, my daughter, do not be afraid, I will do for you all that you ask, for all the assembly of my people know that you are a worthy woman. But now, though it is true that I am a near kinsman, there is another kinsman more closely related than I. Remain this night, and in the

morning, if he will act as next-of-kin for you, good; let him do it. If he is not willing to act as next-of-kin for you, then, as the Lord lives, I will act as next-of-kin for you. Lie down until the morning (Ruth 3:11–13)!

You should be honest about your relationship. When you say yes, it should be yes! When you say no, it should be no! Do not promise to marry a sister without prayerfully thinking it through.

The principle of obedience
Boaz chose to obey God rather than follow human opinion. He recognised that Ruth was the will of God for his life. He married Ruth despite her condition as a widow and foreigner.

The principle of holiness
Boaz did not abuse his position of authority or use his wealth to take advantage of Ruth in her state of vulnerability. He displayed godliness. Of course, Ruth met him at the threshing floor, but he did not soil his testimony. He allowed her to lie down at his feet until morning. He persuaded her to get up before anybody would recognise her. He insisted that it must not be known that a woman came to the threshing floor that night (Ruth 3:14). The implication is that many people may not believe their story. You should be concerned about your Christian testimony. Do not do things that will make people to suspect you or question your integrity.

The principle of seeking family approval
Boaz went up to the city gate to have a discussion with the closest next-of-kin to Elimelech. He also invited ten men of the elders of the city to the meeting. He expressed his willingness to marry Ruth if the next-of-kin is not interested. He also indicated

that he was willing to bear the responsibilities. He took the proper step and sought family approval (Ruth 4:1–6). In a similar vein, it is honourable for you to inform your family (especially your parents) and get their approval. You must take the right step like Boaz.

The principle of making the relationship legal

Boaz took another step after getting the approval of the family. He followed the ancient custom of confirming and attesting to legal transaction in Israel. The next-of-kin took off his sandal and handed it over to Boaz as a piece of evidence (Ruth 4:7–10). In our contemporary context, there should be a legal covenant between you and the lady you want to marry. You are required by law to go to the marriage registry in order to make your relationship valid. Christians also need to do the Church blessing or wedding to make their relationship legal before God and the Church.

The principle of making your relationship public

The city gate where Boaz got the approval to marry Ruth was a public place. Many people in Bethlehem got to know that Ruth and Boaz were engaged.

> Then all the people who were at the gate, along with the elders, said, "We are witnesses. May the Lord make the woman who is coming into your house like Rachel and Leah, who together built up the house of Israel. May you produce children in Ephrathah and bestow a name in Bethlehem; and, through the children that the Lord will give you by this young woman, may your house be like the house of Perez, whom Tamar bore to Judah" (Ruth 4:11–12).

It is important for friends and family members to know about your relationship. This can strengthen your commitment for each other.

Conclusion

Boaz has become a model for unmarried young men, widowers and those who are looking for love. We encourage all young men to begin to apply the principles they have learnt from the life of Boaz in this chapter. They are timeless principles that are still relevant in our contemporary society. Your life cannot remain the same again when you practice them.

God has preserved your wife for you somewhere. You will soon discover her in Jesus name. A young man who is close to our family recently attended the Nigerian National Youth Service Corps (NYSC). He was posted to one of the states affected by Islamist insurgency in the northern part of Nigeria. He was not happy, but he reluctantly reported when he could not change the posting. He met a lady with a dual nationality that also reluctantly reported for her national service there. They became good friends and resolved to get married. They have both migrated to United Kingdom. They are now happily married with a daughter. You will soon have a mind-blowing testimony in Jesus name.

Solution Prayer Points

- I reject every form of temptation that is designed to destroy my life and marital chances in Jesus name.
- Father, satisfy my physical, spiritual and emotional needs in Jesus name.
- Let your word dwell in me richly and keep me from falling in Jesus name.
- My faith and commitment to the Lord shall not be contaminated in Jesus name.
- Give me the grace to occupy myself with godly activities in Jesus name.
- It is finished. Every curse in my life is finished. Every limit on my life and relationship is finished in Jesus name.
- Every evil manipulation of my marital life shall be destroyed in Jesus name.
- My current singleness will end with praise and testimonies in Jesus name.
- I break every covenant concerning late marriage in my life in Jesus name.
- Father Lord, keep me from the mistakes that are designed to rob me of my life partner in Jesus name.
- I break the chain of singleness in my life now in the name of Jesus.
- My vision for marriage will not die; my dream about the future will not be aborted in Jesus name.
- Oh Lord, let your mercy cover every mistake that I have made in the past in Jesus name.
- Those who would disappoint me or ruin my life will not cross my way in Jesus name.
- I reject every satanic offer of a life partner for me in Jesus name.

- I reject every form of frustration and discouragement concerning my marital status in Jesus name.
- Father Lord, let my path cross with the woman that you have ordained for my life in Jesus name.
- I announce my marital breakthrough and deliverance today in Jesus name.
- I shall not struggle in the area of relationship in Jesus name.
- Oh Lord, give me the spirit of discernment before I date anybody in Jesus name.
- Guide me oh Lord in my dating experiences in Jesus name.
- Help me to prepare spiritually before embarking on a date in Jesus name.
- I receive the motivation to spend time with God before making a decision on the one I shall spend the rest of your life with in Jesus name.
- My faith in God shall be strengthened through my marital relationship and not weakened in Jesus name.
- I shall not lack for godly counsel on marriage in Jesus name.

Chapter 3

Relationship Lessons from the Book of Ruth

There are many lessons for us to learn from the book of Ruth that are applicable to contemporary Christians. We have chosen in this book only to focus on the ones applicable to marriage and relationship. We can now glean more from the book because our approach and reflection have opened it up for more possibilities. In this chapter, we shall consider forty-one (41) lessons.

Choose a believer. Apart from being born again, the person you would choose to marry must be born again too. Boaz was a worshipper of Yahweh. He ensured that he married another worshipper of Yahweh. Chilion and Mahlon got it wrong when they married Moabite women. This was a violation of the Law of Moses (Deut. 7:3; 23:3 Ezra 9:2 and Neh. 13:23). Some Jewish commentators suggest that the premature deaths of Chilion and Mahlon were divine judgments upon them for their unlawful relationships. Boaz and Ruth on the other hand got it right. They were both worshippers of Yahweh when they met. It is a pleasant thing to get married in the Lord.

God can use circumstances. God can use circumstances (both good and bad) to direct you to the right partner. It appeared to be a disaster when Ruth lost her husband (Mahlon), but God in his wisdom had a better plan. God can allow or orchestrate a situation to happen if the person you are going out with at the moment is not his will for your life. God eventually resettled Ruth and gave her an important place in the salvation history of humankind. God is working out His own plan through the current circumstances in your life.

Every disappointment is a blessing. Ruth was disappointed when (Mahlon), her first husband died, but it turned out to be a blessing. Have you been disappointed by a brother or sister? God has a way of turning things around in your favour.

With God, a delay is not a denial. People may call it a delay, but it is a design. As we mentioned earlier, the Bible is silent about the marital situation of Boaz because that was not the interest of the biblical narrator. It is not clear whether he had a wife but she died around the same time. Boaz himself may have had a delay in getting married. Biblical scholars have suggested many possibilities in an attempt to answer this question. What we understand from the text is the fact that Boaz was far older than Ruth.

Similarly, we can also argue that Boaz was single at that time. Bush notes that the Mosaic Law required such marriage only when the male survival was legally able to marry his brother's widow. However, he cannot do so if he already had a wife (1996: 221–223). In other words, he does not have to become a polygamist after his brother's death. God brought Ruth and Boaz together so that they could fill the vacuum in the lives of each other. May the Lord lead you to the specific person that will occupy that vacuum in your life in Jesus name!

God can order your steps. Ruth initially went out to glean from the field. The Law of Moses allows the poor and needy, such as aliens, widows and orphans to glean in the field behind the reapers. This will allow them to get some food for their own survival (Lev. 19:9–10; 23:22). The Bible says, 'as it happened, she came to the part of the field belonging to Boaz, who was of the family of Elimelech' (Ruth 2:3). God's providential guidance can lead you to your life partner. The story of Ruth and Boaz shows that getting a life partner requires a divine connection. The Bible says, 'he who finds a wife finds a good thing, and obtains favour from the Lord' (Prov. 18:22). Similarly, God ordered the steps of Boaz. He visited the reapers on the field and saw Ruth there. 'Then Boaz said to his servant who was in charge of the reapers, "To whom does this young woman belong"' (Ruth 2: 4–5)? A divine direction would end up with a divine connection (Bakare, 2014: 20–21). It was a divine direction for Ruth and Boaz. It appeared to be accidental from human perspective, but it was a connection directed by God.

There is hope for a better future. The Bible says, 'the end of a matter is better than it's beginning' (Eccl. 7:8). The beginning may be little and challenging, but it will end in joy. Ruth's husband died but the Lord resettled her. It is not everyone that is labeled a 'senior bachelor' or 'senior girl' that would remain like that forever. God will orchestrate a turn around in your life. You will be happily married in Jesus name. Have a picture in your mind about the day you will meet your life partner, your wedding day and your future children.

Act by faith. Ruth acted by faith and left the consequences to God. She demonstrated a great faith that probably went beyond that of Abraham in Genesis 12. As Hubbard notes, 'she acted with no promise in hand, with no divine blessing pronounced, without spouse, possessions, or supporting retinue. She gave up marriage to a man to devote herself to an old woman' (Hubbard, 1988: 120). You also have a responsibility to act by faith on every issue in life including marriage.

Speak nicely. Boaz spoke nicely to Ruth in all their conversations. He blessed her and used good words to describe her loyalty (Ruth 3:10). Biblical scholars have suggested that it was rare for an Israelite to treat foreigners politely the way Boaz did during the period of the judges. He blessed her because of her unselfish love for Naomi (Ruth 3:11) and her trust in Yahweh (Ruth 3:12).

Don't give up. You must persistently wait upon the Lord. Don't give up about the prospect of getting married. Naomi encouraged Ruth to keep trying. Ruth did not give up. Boaz too did not give up about the prospect of getting married to a God-fearing woman. It eventually happened. The same God can meet your need for a life partner.

God is at work in your life. One of the primary purposes of the book of Ruth is to reveal how God often providentially work behind the scenes to bring His will to pass. God is still at work in your life. He has not forgotten you. According to John Reed, 'the Ruth narrative provided a gratifying reminder that even in the darkest times God was at work in the hearts of His faithful remnant' (1985: 416). God will remember you as He remembered Ruth and Boaz in Jesus name.

God will preserve your partner for you. It is amazing to imagine how God preserved Boaz for Ruth. Boaz lived in Bethlehem while Ruth lived in Moab. Yet God preserved them for each other. The same God can preserve a husband or wife for you in Nigeria, Ghana, South Africa, United Kingdom, United States of America, South America, Canada, Australia, India, Dubai and other parts of the world.

It is possible for you to get a good mother-in-law. The story of Ruth shows that Naomi was a great mother-in-law. God used her to shape the relationship of Ruth and Boaz. She became a model for all mothers-in-law today. According to Reed, 'this is the best of all mother-in-law stories and should be told repeatedly' (1985: 417). God provided a good mother-in-law for Ruth at that time in Israel. He is able to do the same in our spiritually apostate and morally corrupt environment.

Follow godly instruction. Naomi's proposal that Ruth should go to meet Boaz should not be misunderstood. It is in line with Israel's law. As Ross notes, Naomi was not encouraging Ruth to engage in sexual immorality (1987: 79). The phrase 'uncover his feet' (Ruth 3:4) is a reference to the blanket (Ruth 3:15) covering Boaz's legs and feet as he slept at the threshing floor. The request for covering is symbolic (Ruth 3:10). Ruth requested for Boaz's protection (Kruger, 1984: 86). She wanted to know if he would like to be her husband (Deut. 22:30; 27:20; Ezek. 16:8; Mal. 2:16). In other words, Naomi's proposal was an encouragement for Ruth to pursue the possibility of marriage. According to the Nelson Study Bible, 'touching and holding his feet was an act of submission' (1997: 446).

Don't worry. Don't worry about your past or current condition. God will take care of that when you meet the right partner. Ruth was a Moabitess (foreigner). She was a childless widow. She was among the poor in Bethlehem without any prospect. Yet, God used her condition to accomplish His purpose.

You can overcome temptations. Boaz was a wealthy man. He lived at a time of spiritual apostasy when most people were morally corrupt. Nevertheless, he overcame all the temptations through the help of God. Similarly, Ruth was a poor Moabite young woman who would have resulted to prostitution because of her extremely vulnerability. Yet she relied on Yahweh and overcame her temptations. Boaz and Ruth did not allow their circumstances to control their spirituality. You too can be an overcomer like them by trusting in God to see you through.

Don't expect too much too quickly. Ruth did not expect too much too quickly. She took one step at a time. Don't expect too much too quickly after losing your partner through disappointment or death. Over time, the practicalities of life will claim more and more of your attention. You will be able to recover and start a new relationship. Eventually, you will find yourself being able to smile and laugh again.

Prayer is vital. Biblical scholars have observed that most of the prayers in the book of Ruth are connected with blessing. It is amazing that God answered all of them. You must make prayer your priority. Prayer is a vital spiritual exercise if you want to successfully find a life partner. You should enquire of the Lord about who you should marry? When you should marry? Where you should marry? Ask God for clarity on specific areas of your marital relationship. Are you currently disappointed that you have prayed for so long and nothing is happening in your life? Do you feel you are not experiencing the joy and fulfillment you expected at this stage of your life? Are you experiencing fears about the possibility of remaining single in your lifetime? Are you worried that things might go wrong in the future? Are you wondering if your wedding day will ever come? Are you struggling between waiting upon the Lord for a partner and going back to the world? Do what Ruth and Boaz did by taking everything to God in prayer. Praying for a life partner is the first step that you must take before you make any move. As John Bunyan notes, 'you can do more than pray after you've prayed, but you can't do more than pray until you've prayed.'

God is faithful. There is evidence of God's providential guidance in the book of Ruth. The book shows the faithfulness of God in providing a life partner for those who put their trust in Him. It shows that 'the Lord is faithful in His business of loving, superintending, and providentially caring for His people' (Reed, 1985: 418).

God has prepared the man or woman of your dream. 'Now Naomi had a kinsman on her husband's side, a prominent rich man, of the family of Elimelech, whose name was Boaz' (Ruth 2: 1). God prepared Boaz and Ruth for each other. God is at work. He works in ways we cannot see. He has prepared a specific husband or wife. You will meet that person very soon in Jesus name.

You should marry for the right reasons. Ruth and Boaz express willingness to get married for the right reasons. They wanted to fulfill God's holy ordinance of marriage. They also wanted to raise a child in order to 'maintain the dead man's name (Mahlon) and protect his inheritance' (Ruth 4:10). Psychologists believe that there is no behaviour without a reason (the reason may be good or bad). Your motives matter before the Lord. We get a special reward when we do things for the right reasons. But selfish motives usually attract disqualification and judgment. God only gets behind ideas that fulfill His purposes and demonstrate His love for others. Some people want to get married because of money, sexual lust, social influence, connections, immigration, political appointment etc. These are wrong reasons that would not glorify God. You must get married because you know it is the will of God for your life.

It pays to work hard. Ruth's work ethic was exceptional. The head of the reapers reported that Ruth was a hard worker (Ruth 2:7). Boaz also confirmed the same testimony (Ruth 2:11).

Moreover, Ruth continued to glean on the field of Boaz after gaining a maidservant status. She used the gleaning to support whatever income she may have earned from Boaz. The implication is that she has to work from morning till late in the evening. She probably rested for only a short time. This eventually became a point of attraction for Boaz.

Don't blame God. In contrast to Naomi who blamed God for becoming a widow in Ruth chapter one, Ruth did not blame God for her condition. Warren Wiersbe's analysis of Ruth chapter one shows that there are three common mistakes that people usually make in life: 'trying to run from our problems (1:1–5), trying to hide our mistakes (1:6–18), and blaming God for our trials (1:19–22)' (Wiersbe, 2003: 182). It appears that Ruth learnt a lesson from the errors of others because she did not make the same mistake. Therefore, you must learn from the mistakes of those who have made wrong choices around you. You must refuse to follow their error. Don't blame God for your state of singleness. Don't ever think that God is picking on you.

Keep yourself busy. Work can be a lifesaver for those who are trusting God for a life partner. More importantly, your personal involvement in Church activities will help you to think less about the pain of singleness. This can also protect you from unnecessary temptations and evil thoughts.

God can turn a 'nobody' to 'somebody.' Ruth arrived Bethlehem as nobody. She was initially working along with Boaz's maidservants. She eventually became an important figure in Israel and our salvation history. God will perform the same miracle in your life in Jesus name.

God should be at the centre of your relationship. God was the main focus of the relationship between Ruth and Boaz (Ruth 2: 20). No wonder, the end result was great. This is an interesting lesson. God should be the center of any relationship you will ever enter into. God should be the reason for your coming together. He should be the alpha and omega of everything.

God can reward you with a life partner. There is a reward for everything you do. God is faithful. He rewards those who seek him diligently. He offered Ruth to Boaz as a reward for faithfully waiting. The Lord will surely reward you with a godly life partner in Jesus name.

Hand it over to God. Ruth realised that she had no control over her life challenges. She chose to hand it over to God by rejoicing in the Lord regardless of what happened. You have a choice to handle it yourself (like Orpah) or hand it over to God (like Ruth). You can draw from God the strength to carry on when you hand it over. You must discern between what is truly important and what is merely temporal. God may not take you out of that situation but He will surely bring you through it. You should always remember that the God you serve is bigger than the obstacles you face.

The news about you is spreading. The news about you is spreading whether you realise it or not. Boaz told Ruth, 'all that you have done for your mother-in-law since the death of your husband has been fully told me, and how you left your father and mother and your native land and came to a people that you did not know before. May the Lord reward you for your deeds' (Ruth 2: 11–12). It is possible that somebody is about to make a decision to propose to you following your good testimony in the community. On the other hand, those who are interested in you may be discouraged to propose if they hear bad things about you.

Take responsibility for your own happiness. Parents, friends and family members can help you, but in the end you are responsible for your own life. Only you can decide how you want to live your life. Don't be discouraged by side comments about your single status. You must believe in God's report and not the shocking statistics about the unmarried people. You should follow the path of Ruth and Boaz by expressing unspeakable joy in the midst of personal challenges.

You must discover your purpose in life. It may help to ask yourself the following questions: What is my purpose in this world? What really matters to me? Who really matters to me? How do I enjoy spending my time? Where do I want to spend eternity? The answers to these questions will enable you to re-examine yourself and set your priorities right. Your purpose in life is not all about marriage. There are other things that God wants you to accomplish. Ruth and Boaz discovered their purpose by serving God and helping others. They also discovered God's purpose for their marriage.

There is a reason for your test of faith. You may not know the reason why you go through some tests in life but God knows. Ruth did not understand why she lost her husband (Mahlon) at such a tender age. It was a test or trial of faith but it became a testimony. There is a reason for your current state of singleness. There is a point that God wants to use your life to prove.

Be careful. Your divine connection may not appear to you in suit and tie. Your prospective husband or wife may not come in the way you expect. The Jews missed the first advent of Jesus Christ in the first century because he was not born in the house of Herod or other influential rulers at that time. He came in a humble way. Naomi was a poor woman, yet God used her to find a husband for Ruth. God's instrument for orchestrating your life partner may choose to come in an unnoticed way.

You reap what you sow. Ruth showed kindness to Naomi and the Lord used Boaz to reciprocate. Ruth found the favour in the sight of Boaz (Ruth 2: 2, 13). He promoted her from a gleaner to a maidservant and then to a wife. The Lord used Boaz to meet her physical, spiritual and emotional needs. The Bible says, 'be not deceived; God is not mocked: for whatsoever a man soweth, that shall he also reap' (Gal. 6:7).

Stop comparing yourself with others. Boaz and Ruth did not compare themselves with other unmarried people in Bethlehem. It can be intimidating for you when your friends and classmates are getting married. You must remember that God has a unique plan for you. He also has a set time for your marriage. God has planned your marriage for an appointed time, 'if it seems to tarry, wait for it; it will surely come, it will not delay' (Hab. 2:3).

You must be grateful to God. Give thanks to God in every situation. Anyone who is not grateful is a great fool. There is a purpose in your being where you are at the moment. Instead of complaining, start looking for people who need what God has given to you. No matter what state you are today; you are better than someone. Ruth showed her gratitude to God by offering Naomi her time and service. You must go out today and help somebody as your act of gratitude to God.

Blessed is the man or woman who takes notice of you. There are many singles with lots of talents and virtues in our society today, but their prospective partners have ignored them. It is a blessing when somebody notices you. The man or woman who specifically takes notice of your good character and is thinking of getting married to you is also blessed (Ruth 2: 19b). The Bible says, 'he who finds a wife finds a good thing, and obtains favour from the Lord' (Prov. 18:22). On the other hand, whosoever finds a good husband finds a divine favour.

God can guide your steps. When God is at work in your life nobody can stop Him. The meeting of Ruth with Boaz was not by chance or an accident. It was a divine connection. God guided the steps of Ruth to the field belonging to Boaz (Ruth 2: 19). She went out to glean (work), but she got more than what she expected. Boaz was impressed with Ruth's performance that he persuaded her to stay with his maidservants until they have finished all the harvest (Ruth 2: 21–23). Therefore, God can direct your path to cross with your life partner at work, school, Church, friend's house, campground, hospital, bus or train station, stadium and other interesting places.

It is good to wait upon the Lord. There is a process between the time you pray for a life partner and the time your prayers are answered. In other words, it may take time to wait upon the Lord before you meet your partner. This requires patiently waiting. There is a tendency for you to want to rush when you are in need of something. Ruth and Boaz waited on the Lord and it yielded a great result at the end. Your resolution to wait patiently upon the Lord will yield a great dividend for you in Jesus name.

Age differences don't count when there is love. There appears to be age differences or gap between Ruth and Boaz. This however, was not a problem for both of them. There has been a huge debate about the significance of age differences in marriage. Is it correct? Should this be considered? Does it really matter? What are the consequences etc.? Some ladies would not consider a man who is slightly younger than them or too older than them. Some unmarried men would not consider a lady who is too young or slightly older than them. The debate is inconclusive and it is hard to legislate. It is difficult to say whether it is right or wrong. Our verdict is that marriage is a personal decision. Age should not be a barrier if you are convinced it is the will of God and you genuinely love each other. You are free to marry each other as long as you are willing to count the cost before you make any commitment.

Finding a godly partner is a miracle. It takes a miracle for you Ruth and Boaz to identify each other. Similarly, it takes a miracle for you to genuinely recognise or take notice of the bone of your bone and the flesh of your flesh. It takes a miracle for two people of different personality traits and background to walk in love together. Henceforth, receive a similar miracle in Jesus name.

Those who heard about your pain will hear about your gain. Those who looked down on Ruth as a poor widow and migrant in Israel also witnessed her elevation. The rejected one eventually became the selected one. Those who wrote off your chances of getting married will hear that God has blessed you with a godly husband or wife and children in Jesus name.

Conclusion

It is not everyone that is called 'single' or 'senior girl' that will remain like that forever. We can testify to the life of a man of God that we know whose wife died at a crucial time in his pastoral ministry. It was very painful for everyone (especially the pastor and his congregation). He decided to remarry after some time. The woman he married had prayed and waited for many years for a husband, but nobody took notice of her. She eventually became the first lady of that ministry and a source of comfort to the pastor. May the Lord sort out your singleness in his own way in Jesus name!

Solution Prayer Points

- Every form of darkness surrounding my relationship shall give way to the light of Christ in Jesus name.
- I shall enjoy uncommon marital bliss in Jesus name.
- I shall find a place of rest like Ruth and Boaz in Jesus name.
- Many people will hear about my marital testimony and follow the living God that I serve in Jesus name.
- My marital plans will succeed in Jesus name.
- Those who laughed about my singleness shall come to rejoice with me when I'm married in Jesus name.
- God will do something new concerning my marital life in Jesus name.
- By this time next year, I will look back with joy and gladness on my marriage in Jesus name.
- Henceforth, God will take charge as the master of my marital relationship in Jesus name.
- My marriage will become the star among other marriages in Jesus name.
- I shall walk in dominion over marriage and relationship challenges in Jesus name.
- I shall not walk alone in life in Jesus name.
- Marital failure is not my portion in Jesus name.
- God will give me a clear vision and insight about my life partner in Jesus name.
- Every curse surrounding my marital relationship shall be destroyed in Jesus name.

Conclusion

As we come to the end of this book, we want to remind you that the book of Ruth contains principles and strategies that anyone looking for husband or wife today can follow.

Our analysis in this book so far has led us to two important conclusions: On one hand, there is a supernatural element to finding a life partner. In other words, you need God's guidance and divine assistance. On the other hand, there is a human element to the discussion about marriage and relationship. God will not do for you what you are able to do for yourself. It is your responsibility to do your part and leave the rest to the Almighty God.

Your challenge of not getting a life partner at the moment is not greater than the God that is living in you (1 John 4:4). The strength He provides is bigger than the obstacles you face. This is the time for you to be strong in the Lord! If Ruth and Boaz can overcome the challenge of singleness, you also have what it takes to overcome it.

Do you think that your current state of singleness is a setback? We encourage you to reflect again on the story of Ruth and Boaz. What you think is a setback is actually a divine setup that is being orchestrated by the triune God for a greater comeback in your life. The Lord that helped Ruth and Boaz in the book of Ruth to overcome their singleness will help you in Jesus name. The story of the life of Ruth and Boaz had a happy ending. The story of your life too will have a happy ending in Jesus name. May the husband or wife that God will provide for you be a restorer of your life and a nourisher of your old age in Jesus name. Nothing is impossible when God is on your side.

Solution Prayer Points

- Father Lord, help my eyes to see, my ears to hear and my heart to understand before I make a decision on my marriage in Jesus name.
- I shall rise above relationship challenges in Jesus name.
- I shall enjoy a relationship breakthrough instead of breakdown in Jesus name.
- I shall experience a supernatural enlightenment on my marital relationship instead of confusion in Jesus name.
- Every closed door against my marriage shall open up in Jesus name.
- My marital decision shall be instructed and illuminated through the power of the Holy Spirit in Jesus name.
- God will remember me for good and bless me with a life partner in Jesus name.
- I confess and claim all the promises of God for my marital life in Jesus name.
- Lord I thank you because my marital life is settled.
- Lord I thank you for the total victory you have given me.

Bibliography

Bakare, G. & F., *Choosing a Life Partner Without Tears*, Ibadan: Oluseyi Press, 2000.

Bakare, G. & F., *Divine Connections: A Biblical Perspective*, London: Vine Media, 2014.

Block, D.I., 'Judges, Ruth', *The New American Commentary series*, Nashville: Broadman & Holman Publishers, 1999.

Bush, F.W., *Ruth, Esther: Word Biblical Commentary* series. Dallas: Word Books, 1996.

Gottwald, N., *The Hebrew Bible—A Socio-Literary Introduction*, Philadelphia: Fortress Press, 1985.

Hubbard, R.L., 'The Book of Ruth', *New International Commentary on the Old Testament*, Grand Rapids: Eerdmans, 1988.

Jackson, C., The Black Christian Singles Guide to Dating and Sexuality, Grand Rapids: Zondervan, 2009.

Keil, C. F., and Delitzsch, F., 'Joshua, Judges, Ruth', Translated by James Martin, *Biblical Commentary on the Old Testament*, Edinburgh: T & T Clark, 1887.

Reed, J.W., 'Ruth', in Walvoord and R.B. Zuck (eds.), *The Bible Knowledge Commentary: Old Testament*, Wheaton: Scripture Press, 1985.

Ross, A.P., 'The Daughters of Lot and the Daughter-in-Law of Judah: Hubris or Faith in the Struggle for Women's Rights' Exegesis and Exposition 2:1 (1987) 71–82.

The Nelson Study Bible. Edited by Earl D. Radmacher. Nashville: Thomas Nelson Publishers, 1997.

Wiersbe, W.W., *The Bible Exposition Commentary*, Colorado Springs: Cook Communications Ministries, 2003.

Other Spiritual Materials from the Authors

A. Solution Books

- The Christian Youth and Pre-marital Sex
- The Power of Communication in a Christian Home
- The 'Little Little' Things that Matter in Marriage
- Choosing a Life Partner Without Tears
- Listening to God in the Midst of Many Voices
- Overcoming Tension Points in Marriage
- It is Possible
- Inviting Jesus into your Marriage
- Divine Connections: A Biblical Perspective
- Overcoming the Deceptions of Rogue Pastors, Churches and Christians

B. Solution Tapes or CDS

- What is Marriage?
- Beware of the Serpent!
- The Little Things that Matter in Marriage (Part 1)
- The Little Things that Matter in Marriage (Part 2)
- Overcoming Selfishness in Marriage
- Overcoming Stress in Marriage
- The Dynamics of Christian Marriage
- The Significance of Forbearance in Marriage
- Resurrection of Hope
- The Resurrection Power

You can buy any of the above materials online at www.ecwauk.org.uk/bookstore/solution-books/. You can also e-mail: solutionoutreach@yahoo.co.uk or divsolmin1@yahoo.com